ARED (Advanced-Resistive Exercise Device) Update

NASA Technical Reports Server (NTRS), Lori Ploutz-Snyder

Evidence-Based Exercise Prescription for use on the ISS (EB ExRx)

New exercise hardware
- ARED resistance exercise
  - Higher loads (600 vs 150 lbs)
  - More exercises (29 different ones)
  - Instrumented to allow data acquisition – LOADS!
- T2 treadmill
  - Better harness & subject loading system
  - Instrumented to allow ground reaction force data

Basic Changes
- Higher intensity, less exercise time
- 3 days/week resistance exercise
  - 3-12 RM periodized
  - Standard care is 6 days/week
- Aerobic exercise every day
  - Also periodized
  - 30 min continuous on resistance days
  - High intensity intervals on alternate day (15-35 min)

Better physiological outcomes
- Typical medical tests
- Muscle CSA (US/MRI)
- Full battery of muscle function
- VO_2max
- Muscle biopsy option

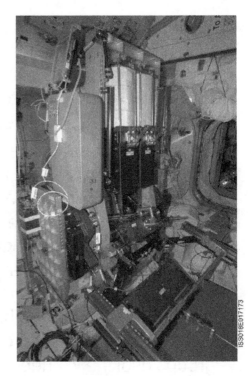

ISS018E017173

3

Specific Aims & Hypotheses

- **Hypothesis 1** – Three days/week of resistance training using ARED at higher intensity will better protect skeletal muscle mass and function, a equally protect bone health compared to resistance exercise on ARED days/week at a lower intensity. Both ARED protocols will be more effective than the IRED exercise program (historic data set).

- **Aim 1** – This hypothesis will be tested by comparing two ARED protocols, the new EB-ExRx and the standard care ExRx care from Space Medicine's Astronaut Strength, Conditioning and Rehabilitation (ASCR) group. Dependent variables under comparison include muscle mass, isometric and isokinetic muscle strength, endurance, power, central activation ratio, single fiber muscle function, oxidative and glycolytic muscle enzymes, and bone mineral density. The new protoco will be compared to the historic IRED data set using only the standard medical tests assessed on all astronauts and thus common to all three groups (isokinetic knee, ankle, back strength, general fitness test, and bone mineral density).

Specific Aims & Hypotheses

Hypothesis 2 – Alternating days of high intensity interval training with days of continuous aerobic exercise will be more effective than predominantly continuous aerobic exercise in the maintenance of cardiovascular function.

Aim 2 – This hypothesis will be tested by comparing the two exercise protocols, the new EB-ExRx and the standard care ExRx care from Space Medicine's Astronaut Strength, Conditioning and Rehabilitation (ASCR) group. Dependent variables under comparison include ventilatory threshold, HR at submaximal workload, and VO2max. The new protocols will be compared to the historic IRED data set using only the standard medical tests that are assessed on all astronauts and thus are common to all three groups (submaximal estimate of VO2max, HR at submax workload).

- **Hypothesis 3** – Recovery of muscle function and VO2max will be most rapid in the EB-ExRx group, followed by standard care, followed by historic ISS group (who used ol exercise hardware).

- **Aim 3** – Two different analyses will be performed to evalua this hypothesis. First, all 3 groups will be compared using t standard medical tests common to all 3 groups. The EB-ExRx and standard care groups will be compared using standard medical data plus the new measures unique to th project.

Important Bone Parameters

High magnitude (Rubin & Lanyon, 1985) **and rate of dynamic (not static) strain** (Hsieh & Turner, 2001).

Diverse strain distributions as bone adaptations are well documented to be site specific in humans as evidenced by both *in vitro* (Bass et al., 2002) and *in vivo* investigations (Maple et al, 1997; Winters-Stone & Snow, 2006).

Only a **few repetitions are required** (Rubin & Lanyon, 1984).

Multiple daily exercise sessions optimize bone growth (Robling et al., 2000**).**

Longer rest intervals between sessions and sets is beneficial (Robling et al., 2001).

Important Muscle Parameters

- Evidence for maintaining muscle mass and function during flight analogs comes from over 25 bedrest and ULLS published studies.
- Flywheel, LBNP treadmill, traditional weights
- Effective studies ALL used maximal or nearly maximal contractions

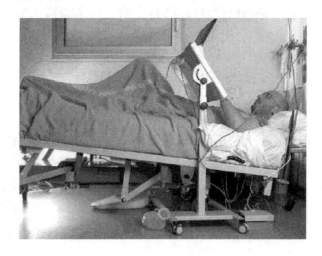

Intensity most important single factor affecting training maintenance

10 week high intensity training (90-100% max HR) interval cycle (6x 5min, 2 min rest) exercise alternated with continuous running as fast as possible for 30 min.

After 10 weeks one training parameter was manipulated to see whether fitness could be maintained over the next 15 weeks with reductions in either exercise intensity, duration or frequency (Hickson et al, 1981, 1982, 1985).

Intensity – decreased 1/3 or 2/3 in WR

Duration – decreased from 40 min/day to 26 or 13

Frequency - decreased from 6 day/week to 4 or 2

Hickson Study Results

- Physiological adaptations were most robust to a decrease training frequency as evidenced by a maintained VO_2max with as little as 2 days/week of high intensity exercise.

- Most physiological adaptations were maintained despite a decreased exercise duration, even with as little as 13 min/day of training. The exception was that long-term (~2h endurance was not maintained in the shortest duration (13 min/day) group, however short term (~5 min) endurance w maintained.

- Despite training 6 days/week for 40 min/day VO_2max, long-term endurance, and left ventricular mass were not maintained with as little as a one-third reduction in training workrate. Alarmingly, all increases in left ventricular mass observed from the initial 10 weeks of training were completely lost when workrate was reduced by one-third.

So What?

The application of this work to the current proposal suggests that **to minimize crew time spent on exercise, that exercise frequency and duration may be reduced but intensity must be maintained at as high of levels as reasonably possible.**

Current Exercise on ISS

- Current in-flight aerobic exercise consists of 30-40 min of continuous exercise at 70-85% of maximal heart rate (HRmax) with treadmill running at less than 1 full body weight of resistance.

- Research literature overwhemingly shows the greatest benefits in markers of cardiorespiratory fitness are realized with higher intensity (85-100%), lower duration exercise protocols such as intermittent or interval programs combining short sprints with short to medium rest periods f a wide variety of populations ranging from heart disease patients to endurance athletes (example reviews Gibala & McGee, 2007; Meyer et al, 1998; Midgley & McNaughton, 2006).

Intervals

20-30 second intervals. The shortest well documented protocols are 20-30 sec "all out" sprints such as those described by Tabata et al. and Gibala et al.

dramatic increases in muscle oxidative capacity including increased oxidative enzymes citrate synthase and cytochrome oxidase, increased markers of mitochondrial carbohydrate (pyruvate dehydrogenase E1alpha protein content) and lipid (3-hydroxacyl CoA dehydrogenase) oxidation, and activation of signaling cascades linked to mitochondrial biogenesis (AMPK and p38MAPK).

- **2 minute intervals.** There are many studies documenting the effectiveness of 2 minute interval aerobic exercise programs for improving cardiovascular function. Importantl there are a series of bedrest studies utilizing interval LBNF treadmill exercises (3 min stages at 60-80% VO2max) that show a maintenance of VO2 max and sprint speed over 3C days of bedrest (Lee et al., 2008)

4 minute and longer intervals. There is a large body of literature documenting the superiority of 4 minute high intensity intervals to continuous exercise in training induced CV adaptations especially in special populations.

Intervals Selected

- **Intensified Greenleaf** - 5 minute warm up at 50% VO2max, followed by 6x2 minute stages at 70, 80, 90, 100, 90%, 80% VO2max. The first 5 stages are separated by 2 minute active rest stages at 50% VO2 max. The final stage is a 5 min active rest at 40% VO2max.

- **Short Sprint** - 10 minute warm up at 50% of HRmax, followed by 7-sets of maximal exercise for 30 seconds, followed by 15 seconds rest. Increase load after 9 sets

- **4 minute** - 5 minute warm up at ~50% HRmax, followed by intervals exercise at 90% HRmax. The exercise intervals will be 4x4 min bouts, with 3 min active rest periods

Intervals

Day 2 / Protocol 1	Day 4 / Protocol 2	Day 6 / Protocol 3
6 x2 minute stages at 70, 80, 90, 100, 90, 80% VO_2max with 2 min rest in between; >50% of sessions on T2 = 32 min total time	8 x 30 sec at maximal effort with 15 sec rest in between – all sessions passive treadmill =15 min total	4x4 min at 90% HRmax with 3 min active rest; >50% of sessions on T2 = 35 min total

EB-ExRx
Resistance

Weekly Training Schedule

	Day 1	Day 2	Day 3
	Squat, Bench Press, Romanian Dead Lift, Upright Row, Heel Raise	Dead Lift, Shoulder Press, Single Leg Squat, Bent-over Row, Single Leg Heel Raise	Front Squat, Bent-over Row, Sumo Dead Lift, Bench Press, Heel Raise
Week			
1	Light	Light	Light
2	Light	Moderate	Light
3	Moderate	Light	Heavy
4	Moderate	Light	Moderate
5	Heavy	Moderate	Light
6	Moderate	Light	Heavy
7	Light	Heavy	Moderate
8	Heavy	Light	Heavy
9	Moderate	Heavy	Moderate
10	Heavy	Light	Moderate
11	Heavy	Moderate	Light
12	Moderate	Light	Heavy

EB-ExRx
Resistance

Program Variables for the Resistance Training Intervention

Weeks 1-6			
	Light	Moderate	Heavy
Sets	3	3	3
Reps	12	8-10	6-7
Rest (sec)	90	120	120
Total Time (min)	35	40	40
Weeks 7-12			
	Light	Moderate	Heavy
Sets	3	4	4
Reps	12	6-8	3-5
Rest (sec)	90	150	180
Total Time (min)	35	50	60

Integration

	Day 1	Day 2	Day 3	Day 4	Day 5	Day 6	Da
Resistance	35-60 min		35-60 min		35-60 min		
Aerobic Interval		32 min		15 min		35 min	
Aerobic Continuous	30 min		30 min		30 min		

Preferably 8 hours, but at least 4 hours will separate exercise bouts
Time savings – 3 hr/week

Outcome Measurements

Muscle CSA
- Pre/Post-flight MRI
- Pre/In/Post-flight Ultrasound

Muscle Function FTT

Single fiber size, contractile function, type

Aerobic & glycolytic enzymes
- Citrate synthase & PFK

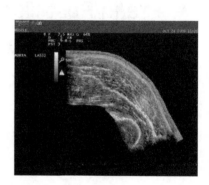

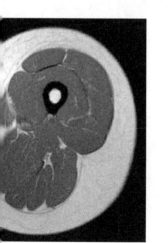

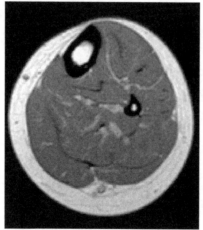

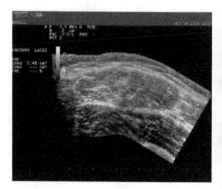

CV

- Pre/In/Post-flight VO2max
- Ventilatory threshold pre/post-flight
- HR response to submax load pre/in/post

Standard Medical

Bone – DEXA or qCT

Isokinetic (quad, calf, back)

Functional fitness

Submax VO2 test

Test Schedule

Time	Test	Time Required
Preflight L<365	Bone	60 min
Preflight L-180	Isokinetic knee, ankle, back	75 min
Preflight L-60-90	Isokinetic knee, ankle, back	60 min
Preflight L-45-50	Biopsy	60 min
Preflight L-30-35	MRI, Muscle, US, VO_2max	60, 50, 30, 60 min
Postflight R+0	US, Biopsy	30 min, 60 min
Postflight R+2	Muscle, VO_2max	50, 60 min
Postflight R+5	Isokinetic knee, ankle, functional fit	60,60 min
Postflight R+6	MRI, Muscle, US	60, 40, 30 min
Postflight R+10	VO_2max	60 min
Postflight R+14	Isokinetic knee, ankle, back	60 min
Postflight R+29	Muscle, VO_2max	40, 60 min
Postflight R+30	Isokinetic knee, ankle, back, functional fit	60, 60 min
Postflight <R+30	Bone	60 min